## EXPLORING WORLD CULTURES

# South Africa

Kate Shoup

Cavendish
Square

New York

Published in 2018 by Cavendish Square Publishing, LLC
243 5th Avenue, Suite 136, New York, NY 10016

Library of Congress Cataloging-in-Publication Data

Names: Shoup, Kate, 1972- author.
Title: South Africa / Kate Shoup.
Other titles: Exploring world cultures.
Description: New York : Cavendish Square Publishing, 2018. |
Series: Exploring world cultures
Identifiers: LCCN 2016046356 (print) | LCCN 2016046741 (ebook) |
ISBN 9781502625076 (pbk.) | ISBN 9781502625083 (6 pack) | ISBN 9781502625090
(library bound) | ISBN 9781502625106 (E-book)
Subjects: LCSH: South Africa--Juvenile literature. |
South Africa--Civilization.
Classification: LCC DT1719 .S56 2017 (print) | LCC DT1719 (ebook) |
DDC 968--dc23
LC record available at https://lccn.loc.gov/2016046356

Editorial Director: David McNamara
Editor: Kristen Susienka
Copy Editor: Rebecca Rohan
Associate Art Director: Amy Greenan
Designer: Joseph Macri
Production Coordinator: Karol Szymczuk
Photo Research: J8 Media

Printed in the United States of America

# Contents

| | | |
|---|---|---|
| **Introduction** | | 4 |
| Chapter 1 | Geography | 6 |
| Chapter 2 | History | 8 |
| Chapter 3 | Government | 10 |
| Chapter 4 | The Economy | 12 |
| Chapter 5 | The Environment | 14 |
| Chapter 6 | The People Today | 16 |
| Chapter 7 | Lifestyle | 18 |
| Chapter 8 | Religion | 20 |
| Chapter 9 | Language | 22 |
| Chapter 10 | Arts and Festivals | 24 |
| Chapter 11 | Fun and Play | 26 |
| Chapter 12 | Food | 28 |
| **Glossary** | | 30 |
| **Find Out More** | | 31 |
| **Index and About the Author** | | 32 |

# Introduction

South Africa is at the southern tip of Africa. That is why it is called *South* Africa. People have lived there for thousands of years. In 1652, people from Europe started taking over the land. In 1934, South Africa became a country.

For many years, white South Africans and black South Africans lived separately. Black South Africans did not have as many rights as white South Africans. This was called **apartheid**. It was wrong. In 1994, South Africa passed a new set of laws, called a constitution. It gave everyone the same rights. South Africans also chose its first black president, Nelson Mandela.

Today, South Africa has eleven official languages. Many people in South Africa speak more than one language.

Most South Africans live in cities. These cities are very modern. Others live in villages. A lot of wild animals live outside the cities. These include lions and giraffes. South Africa is an exciting place to explore.

A South African woman wears traditional dress.

South Africa sits at the tip of Africa. It is 471,443 square miles (1,221,037 square kilometers). It has a long coast. One part of the coast is by the Atlantic Ocean. The other is by the Indian Ocean.

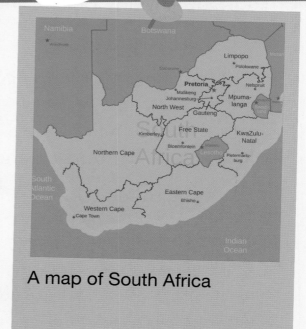

A map of South Africa

The Great **Escarpment** splits the country in two. An escarpment is a steep hill. Along the bottom of the hill is the country's coastal region. The Cape Fold Mountains cover part of this area. Wild animals like lions, rhinoceroses, and giraffes live in another part.

## Plant Life in South Africa

There are very few forests in South Africa. Still, more than twenty thousand types of plants grow there.

A large **plateau** is on top of the escarpment. The east side of the plateau is wet. There are many farms there. The west side is drier. Farther north lies the Kalahari Desert.

Giraffes live in South Africa

## FACT!

Winter in South Africa goes from June to August. Even in winter, the weather stays warm.

Humans have lived in South Africa for more than 100,000 years. In time, they formed groups, called tribes, such as the Bantu, Xhosa, and Zulu.

Africans fought hard to keep their land but were defeated.

Europeans first sailed around the southern tip of South Africa in 1487. In 1652, the Dutch built a fort there. More Dutch settlers arrived soon after.

The British captured South Africa in 1806. European settlers took over more land. African tribes living there fought hard to keep their land. They were defeated.

**FACT!**

In 1948, South Africa passed a system of laws called apartheid that put black citizens under the control of whites. Today, blacks and whites have equal rights.

South Africa became its own country in 1934, but it was still ruled by the British. In 1961, it became independent.

## Nelson Mandela

During apartheid, Nelson Mandela spent twenty-seven years in prison. After apartheid, he was let out and became the country's first black president.

Nelson Mandela

9

VOTE!

South Africa is a **republic**. Its government has three parts:

1. Legislative: Parliament is the legislative part. Parliament writes new laws. It is split into two groups. One is the National Council. It has ninety members. The

South Africa's parliament building in Cape Town

other is the National Assembly. It has four hundred members.

2. Executive: The president is head of the executive branch. This branch passes new laws.

10

3. Judicial: The courts make up the judicial part of the government. They make sure laws are followed.

South Africa's constitution lists the country's basic laws. Its current constitution was written in 1994.

## Three Capitals

South Africa has three capital cities. One is Pretoria. The executive branch is there. Another is Bloemfontein. The judicial branch is there. Finally, the legislative branch is in Cape Town.

# The Economy

South Africa has the second-largest **economy** in Africa. Mining is one important industry. Mining started in the 1800s. That was when diamonds and gold were found. After that, many South Africans became miners. Some

South Africa's money is very colorful.

South Africans still work as miners today. Many of them mine coal. Mining helped the country grow.

**Tourism** is another important industry. Many people visit South Africa to see its beaches and its wild animals. Tourism brings a lot of money into the country.

A few people in South Africa are very rich, but many more are very poor. Twenty-five percent of South Africans do not have jobs. Some must live on less than $1.25 per day.

## The World's Largest Diamond

The world's largest diamond was found in South Africa. It weighed more than 1 pound (0.45 kilograms). It was cut into several smaller stones. The largest of these is called the Star of Africa.

South Africa has many environmental problems. One is that much of the land is very dry. There is not much fresh water. A lot of the water they do have is dirty.

South Africa buries much of its garbage in landfills.

The air in South Africa is also dirty. One part of South Africa, called the Highveld, has some of the dirtiest air in the world. This is because many South Africans drive cars. They also burn a lot of coal to make electricity.

One reason the air and water are dirty is mining. Waste from mines poisons the water. Dust and smoke from mines pollute the air.

South Africa buries much of its garbage in landfills. These landfills are almost full. This is a big problem.

## Cleaning Up the Environment

South Africa is working to clean up its air and water. For example, South Africans have started using more solar power. Also, South Africans have begun to recycle their trash.

Runoff from mines poisons some of the water in South Africa.

# The People Today

Almost fifty-two million people live in South Africa. Every year, the population grows larger.

The majority of South Africans are black. About one out of every ten South Africans are white. In addition, about one out of ten South Africans are of mixed race. There is also a small

Johannesburg is the biggest city in South Africa.

South Africa has the fifth-largest population in Africa. It has the twenty-sixth-largest population in the world.

Indian population. During apartheid, blacks had fewer rights than whites. Today, they have the same rights.

People in South Africa don't live as long as people in the United States. People in the United States usually live to be almost eighty. People in South Africa usually live only until age sixty-two.

## Where Do South Africans Live?

Over two-thirds of South Africans live in cities. More people move to cities every year. The biggest city is called Johannesburg. More than nine million people live there.

# Lifestyle

Cities in South Africa are very modern. Living in a city in South Africa is like living in one in the United States. People use cars or trains to get around.

Life is different in the countryside. It is more old-fashioned. Many people living there are farmers.

South African cities are very modern.

## FACT!

Members of the same family often live together. A South African boy or girl might live with their parents and many other relatives.

## Tribal Ties

Many people in South Africa are members of a tribe. The largest tribe is the Zulu tribe. The Xhosa tribe is second largest. There are many more tribes. Each tribe has its own traditions and speaks its own language.

Members of the Zulu tribe dance and sing.

Women in South Africa have the same rights as men, but South Africa is largely a **patriarchy**. That means men make many of the decisions. This is especially true in the countryside. Women are trying to become more equal.

# Religion

Before Europeans came to South Africa, each tribe had its own religion. Some people worshipped many gods and goddesses. Others believed in just one god. Today, some South Africans still follow

A church in South Africa

these old religions. Others follow Islam, Judaism, and Hinduism. Most South Africans are Christians.

## FACT!

Europeans converted many African people to Christianity when they arrived in South Africa. Sometimes they did this by force.

When they are sick, many South Africans see a healer called a *sangoma* or an *inyanga*. These healers use traditional African religious rituals to cure the sick.

A South African healer

## Freedom of Religion

Even though most South Africans are Christian, South Africa is a **secular** country. That means people are free to follow any religion they wish. Or they can follow no religion at all. This right is granted by the South African constitution.

# Language

South Africa has eleven official languages. These are listed in the country's constitution. An official language is one that has special status. Most of South Africa's official languages are African languages. These include Zulu and Xhosa.

All eleven official languages appear on the Constitutional Court building.

## What Is Afrikaans?

Afrikaans is a language that grew out of the Dutch language. Dutch was spoken by many early settlers in South Africa.

**Most South Africans speak more than one language. Few can speak all eleven, however.**

Some of these languages are spoken more than others. Zulu is spoken the most. Xhosa and Afrikaans are second-most popular. English is ranked fourth. Many businesspeople and scientists in South Africa must learn how to speak English.

Some words in African languages use different sounds from ours. One of these sounds is a clicking sound.

The African languages used to be spoken but not written down. Now, they are written using the same letters used in English. These letters are called the Latin alphabet.

Art, music, and dance are very important to South Africans. South Africa has many artists. They use all kinds of materials. For example, some artists use recycled items like bicycle parts or soda cans in their art.

Cave paintings in South Africa feature drawings of ancient Africans.

## FACT!

The oldest piece of art ever found was in South Africa. It is a necklace made of shells. It is seventy-five thousand years old.

Early South Africans did not write. Today, there are many South African writers. They write stories and poetry.

Music is very important in South Africa. So is dancing. Many South African tribes perform rituals with music and dancing. There are many festivals to celebrate music and dance.

## South African Holidays

South Africans celebrate several holidays. One is Human Rights Day (March 21). Another is Freedom Day (April 27). A third one is the Day of Reconciliation (December 16). All three of these holidays celebrate the end of apartheid.

# Fun and Play

South Africans like playing and watching sports. Soccer, called football in South Africa, is very popular. There are many famous South African players.

South Africans also like rugby. Many people play this sport.

South African soccer fans cheer during a match.

## FACT!

In 2010, South Africa held the FIFA World Cup. That's the most important soccer tournament in the world. It happens once every four years.

The third most popular sport in South Africa is cricket. Cricket is a little bit like baseball. Players use a ball and a bat to play.

## The 1995 Rugby World Cup

Under apartheid, black and white rugby players could not play together. After apartheid, Nelson Mandela worked with the captain of the national rugby team, Francois Pienaar, to mix the team. That team won the 1995 Rugby World Cup, which was played in South Africa. Mandela presented the trophy to Pienaar. This was a very important event in South African history.

# Food

Traditional African food is very popular in South Africa. African food has a lot of vegetables. One is corn. South Africans use corn to make a porridge called *mealie pap*.

A South African braai

## Meals with Meat

South Africans like meat. They eat beef, chicken, lamb, and pork. They even eat ostrich! Often, they have friends over for a *braai*. That's another word for barbecue. Meat costs a lot of money. That makes it a special treat for some South Africans.

**FACT!**

South Africans eat lots of different kinds of food. This is because the country's population is made up of people from different places.

When Europeans came to South Africa, they brought new kinds of food. This included sausages, meat pies, and different types of fish. Indians who moved to South Africa also brought new kinds of food, such as samosas.

South Africans enjoy a special tea called rooibos tea. It is made from the leaves of a plant that grows in the area.

# Glossary

**apartheid**    A system of laws that put black citizens under the control of whites.

**economy**    The part of a country that deals with the making and selling of goods and services.

**escarpment**    A steep hill.

**patriarchy**    A society in which men are in charge.

**plateau**    A flat area of land on top of a slope.

**republic**    A country governed by elected people rather than a king or queen.

**secular**    A word that describes something that is not religious in nature.

**tourism**    An industry of visitors to the country.

# Find Out More

## Books

Barfield, Cecilia, and Gill Gordon. *All About South Africa*. Cape Town, SA: Penguin Random House South Africa, 2016.

Gifford, Clive. *Unpacked: South Africa*. London: Wayland, 2017.

## Website

**TIME for Kids Around the World: South Africa**

http://www.timeforkids.com/destination/south-africa/day-in-life

## Video

**National Geographic: Destination: South Africa**

http://video.nationalgeographic.com/video/destinations/southafrica-overview-dest

Watch this video to learn all about South Africa's wildlife.

# Index

apartheid, 4, 9, 17,
  25, 27
language, 5, 19, 22–23
Mandela, Nelson, 4,
  9, 27

patriarchy, 19
plateau, 7
religion, 20–21
republic, 10
secular, 21

# About the Author

**Kate Shoup** has written more than thirty-five books and has edited hundreds more. When not working, Shoup loves to ski, read, ride her motorcycle, and watch IndyCar races. She lives in Indianapolis, Indiana, with her husband, her daughter, and their dog.